BREAKING THE STATUS QUO: INFORMATION AND THE FUTURE FORCE

Information is the oxygen of the modern age. It seeps through the walls topped by barbed wire, it wafts across the electrified borders....

—Ronald Reagan[1]

From the earliest recorded times, armed force and aggression have been used to pursue individual, group and nation-state objectives. From the history of Thucydides to the theories of Sun Tzu and Clausewitz to the capability advocating of Douhet, Mahan, and Brodie, military force as an element of national power has been seen as a critical – sometimes the preferred – means to secure national interests. However, the 21st century has seen the emergence of globalization, of economic interdependence, and information availability that has caused the role of military force, and even war, as an instrument of national power to diminish. Clausewitz's theory that "War is ... a continuation of political activity by other means" [2] implies that war is a natural progression in a state's desire to pursue and protect national interests. In the 21st century environment of globalization, military power, and the ability to wage and sustain armed conflict, will take a secondary preference to the application of informational, economic, and cyber capabilities to achieve effects in the operational environment. As nation-states and non-nation actors pursue and protect national, socio-demographic, and niche interests, the military will be required to change how it treats information and how it approaches the application of information as an element of combat power if it is to remain a viable element of national power

The purpose of this paper is to examine how the military leverages and applies information in the pursuit of national objectives, and to recommend changes to military Doctrine, Organization, Training, Materiel, Leader Development and Education,

Personnel, and Facilities (DOTMLPF) necessary to ensure the military is able to meet the strategic needs of the nation. As the global environment becomes increasingly complex and ambiguous, the manner in which the military deters attacks, and when necessary, fights and wins the nation's wars must transform. The potential for force on force conflict between nation-states will continue to diminish, at least among the great powers, while conflicts in the information environment and cyberspace continue to rise. The military must transform its capabilities, and means of applying these capabilities, in order to maintain and increase the ability to achieve the desired effects in these environments. In the past, achieving effects such as "destroy" or "defeat" characterized the employment of military capabilities. In the current and future operational environment, it will be necessary for the military to be able to achieve effects such as informing, influencing, educating and inspiring specific audiences; degrading adversarial information systems and cyber capabilities; and defending friendly information systems. This paper will examine the use of information and economics as elements of national and military power, changes in military's focus on information, the relationship of cyberspace and the information environment, the emergence of cyberspace and cyberspace operations, the evolution of information operations, the emergence of Strategic Communication as a means of coordinating the application of Information, and current application and emerging trends in the fields of Information Operations and Strategic Communication in order to develop and recommend solutions for the military.

The Rise of Information and Economics as Elements of National Power

In his seminal work On War, Carl von Clausewitz defines war as "an act of force to compel our enemy to do our will," and he describes physical force as "the means of war; to impose our will on the enemy is its object." [3] This belief in the ultimate

2

necessity of force and war is not surprising when taken in the context in which Clausewitz was writing. Clausewitz lived in a time in which dynastic warfare was being overtaken by a theory of total war – war in which nations mobilized an entire population to secure their interests. Military power and the threat of its use were seen as the means to secure economic security and diplomatic alliances.

Clausewitz recognized, and advocated, that war was and should be subordinate to national policy. [4] However, 19th century European leaders had fewer viable options at their disposal with which to pursue or secure national interests. Access to information was limited to the comings and goings of diplomatic couriers, spies, and rumors; information as an element of power was in such a nascent state as to be essentially ineffective. In the context of Clausewitz's time, economic influence, the final element of national power, was viewed as the means to raise armies and support military power, not to meet the needs of the citizenry. As a result of these limitations, European leaders were left to rely on military power, the threat of force, and alliances based on the perception of power to meet their national objectives.

The global landscape of the 20th century was vastly different from that in which Clausewitz lived and wrote. The world in which Clausewitz wrote was at the birth of the industrial revolution, an age dominated by "a many-sided social system that touched every aspect of human life and attacked every feature of the First Wave past;"[5] if the First Wave of civilization expansion was a result of the invention of agriculture, then the Second Wave was the child of the industrial revolution. The invention of the telegraph connected societies around the country and across the globe; Marconi and his wireless radio delivered news and entertainment directly into people's homes; newspapers were able to report on global events almost instantaneously; and movies – talking pictures – emerged as a means to not only entertain but also to inform and influence audiences.

From the onset of World War II, even as the United States was gearing up to enter the global contest, the attitudes, beliefs, and behaviors of the American public were constantly shaped by an information campaign that encompassed all aspects of American life. The President passed information to the American public through weekly "fire-side chats." Americans were encouraged to grow "Victory Gardens," lead scrap metal drives, and buy War Bonds. Hollywood rolled out Movietone news releases before every cinema offering, and stalwarts such as Frank Capra produced films destined to stir American patriotism. With these industrial age advances in the ability to share information and communicate came a need to understand audiences, to understand how to inform or inspire different groups. In the 1950s, President Eisenhower, shaped by his wartime experiences in Europe, understood the importance of information and the power it had to shape world affairs. Information warfare was a cornerstone of his Cold War policy, and the nation saw a move from propaganda-type agencies to an all out effort to reach the hearts and minds of populations around the world. Eisenhower believed that "As a nation, everything we say, everything we do, and everything we fail to say or do, will have its impact in other lands."[6]

The advances of the industrial age saw equal advances in the influence of economics and information on national interests. In his farewell address President Eisenhower acknowledged the economic impact of the military industrial complex on the power America wielded as a nation, and he cautioned America on the need to understand the implications incumbent to this economic relationship.[7]   President

Barrack Obama identified the strength of the American economy as the foundation for its strength around the world.[8] The powers of economic influence and access to information now drive the preservation of national interests similar to the manner in which military power and force influenced world leaders of the 19th century. The differences between the world of the 19th century and that of the 21st century go far beyond just the evolution of the national power elements.   For three hundred years industrialization dominated the world stage, until the technological advances of the Third Wave overtook industrialization for primacy in the world system. As Alvin Toeffler wrote in *The Third Wave*, "This new civilization, as it challenges the old, will topple bureaucracies, reduce the role of the nation-state, and give rise to semi-autonomous economies in a post-imperialistic world." [9]

Changing the Military's Focus on Information

In January 2012, President Barrack Obama and Secretary of Defense Leon Panetta issued new strategic guidance to the Department of Defense, directing the department to shift its focus from wars in Afghanistan and Iraq to the importance of the Asia/Pacific region and the emergence of China as a potential challenge to U.S. national interests.[10] Because of globalization, China's seemingly immense influence, and potential threat, over the United States is actually limited. As John Paul Getty said, "If you owe the bank $100, that's your problem. If you owe the bank $100 million, that's the bank's problem." Globalization has ensured a world system in which economic interdependence is everyone's problem and everyone's salvation. Mutually Assured Economic Dependence inhibits states from using military force to secure their national interests – no longer must nation-states occupy a hostile land and its population as was the case during wars of conquest. In the May 2010 *National Security Strategy,*

President Barrack Obama acknowledges this new world system: "the specter of nuclear war has lifted; major powers are at peace; the global economy has grown; commerce has stitched the fate of nations together." [11]

As globalization brings nations closer together, terrorist groups, third-party actors, and states that do not adhere to international treaties and standards will continue to threaten national interests, and the manner in which we prepare for, and address, these threats must change. The National Defense Strategy acknowledges this threat transformation and the necessity to secure global economic well-being through the ability to operate in and through cyberspace.[12] In this era of globalization, an era brought about the emergence of the Third Wave civilization, the need is significantly reduced for standing armies to exist as a physical deterrence to armed attack. National interests are less likely to be secured by traditional military force or the threat of violence. As globalization has brought about the interdependence of nations, so too has it brought about a change to the manner in which nation-states wage war. In a globalized world economy, it is not the military that reigns supreme as an element of national power. Wise leaders who recognize this, who invest in diplomacy, economic, and informational capabilities, will ensure their national interests are best secured. And militaries that understand the power of information, the need to protect the use of it and the ability to wield it as a means for achieving effects, will be better postured to defend their nations.

The Rise of Cyber Capabilities in the Information Environment

In 2007, *The London Times* reported that Israel had developed extensive plans to conduct a limited nuclear strike on Iranian nuclear development capabilities.

Although these planned strikes would be small (one-fifteenth the size of the "Little Boy" atomic bomb used on Hiroshima), the intent was clear: Israel would not allow Iran to become a nuclear power.[13] As a result of this reporting, international pressure weighed in and Israel has yet to follow through on this plan. In July 2010, Iran discovered, through the help of a Belarusian anti-virus company, a computer virus now known as "Stuxnet." Stuxnet had spread through computer operated centrifuges created by the German company Siemens – essential to the production of fissionable nuclear material – and destroyed over 1,000 centrifuges, setting back Iranian nuclear research for many years.[14] Without any physical destruction, without any loss of life, without the civilian population being endangered, Iran's nuclear research program was ground to a halt. At the time of the Stuxnet discovery, it was generally accepted that five nation-states had the ability to develop a virus capable of doing what Stuxnet accomplished: The United States, Russia, China, France, and Israel. Although Israel never claimed responsibility for Stuxnet, nor could Iran prove Israeli or U.S. culpability, the effect accomplished what Israel needed: Iranian nuclear ambitions were severely impeded without the unifying Muslim support for the Iranian regime that would have resulted from a physical attack able of delivering comparable results. The implication of this incident is clear: a nation-state no longer needs to rely on physically destructive acts, delivered by military force, to secure its national interests.

The advent and consistent advancement of cyber-technologies have significantly impacted how a nation, and its military, uses information. For many years various factions in the military debated what exactly cyberspace is: a capability that can be used for operations? A medium through which information can be passed, stored, retrieved, or manipulated? A tool that enables effects to be achieved? The Department of Defense seemingly put the debate to rest in 2008 by defining Cyberspace as "a global domain within the information environment consisting of the interdependent network of information technology infrastructures, including the Internet, telecommunications networks, computer systems, and embedded processors and controllers."[15] With this definition cyberspace became an operational domain, subordinate to the information environment, on par with the land, sea, air, and space domains. Figure 1 below graphically depicts the relationship of cyberspace to the other operational domains.

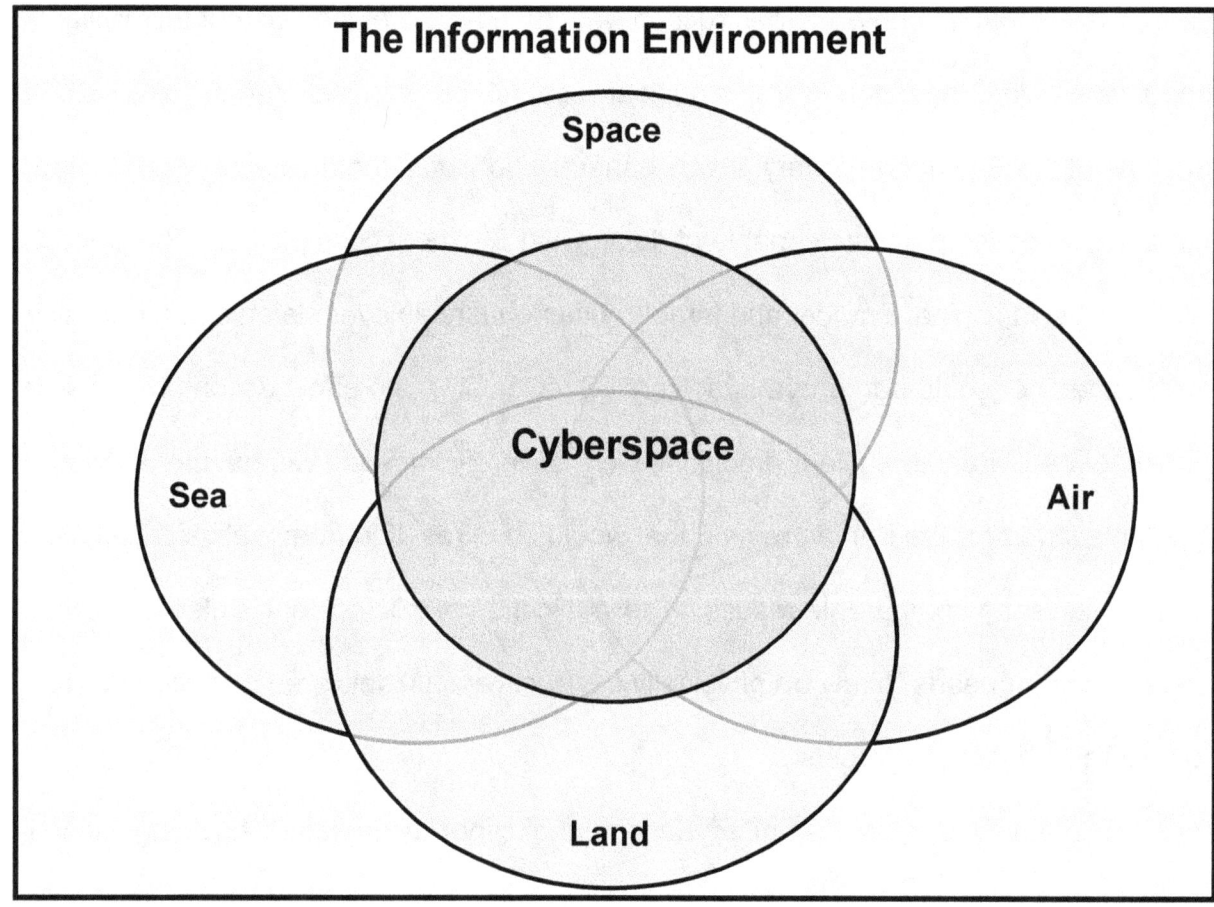

Figure 1: Relationship of the operational domains in the information environment

Just as in the physical domains, military forces could use capabilities to generate effects in the cyber domain. The Joint Chiefs of Staff solidified this conceptualization of cyberspace as an operational domain by defining cyberspace operations as "the employment of cyber capabilities where the primary purpose is to achieve military objectives or effects in or through cyberspace. Such operations include computer network operations and activities to operate and defend the Global Information Grid."[16]

The twenty-first century saw a dramatic shift in the global threats to the United States. Gone were the peer competitors who could threaten the U.S. using a conventional application of the military element of national power. As the U.S. consolidated its global hegemony, the threats and challenges to its national interests adopted asymmetric and unconventional forms. Islamic extremists used terror to strike at our interests at home and abroad while computer hackers attempted to invade our information infrastructure for personal amusement, financial gain, and to support potential adversaries. Recognizing this new threat, President George W. Bush declared that protecting cyberspace, and the public/private infrastructure it served, was essential to American national interests.[17]

The Emergence of Cyberspace and Cyberspace Operations

Although the Department of Homeland Security is charged by the White House to lead U.S. efforts in the defense of cyberspace due to the public-private nature of the environment, the Department of Defense plays a crucial role in the Interagency effort to secure the cyber environment from malicious threats. *The National Military Strategy for Cyberspace Operations*, released by the Secretary of Defense in December 2006, outlines the critical importance access to cyberspace plays for military options and the necessity to preserve this access. It directs the Department of Defense to develop the capability and capacity necessary to execute the full range of military operations both in and through cyberspace.[18]

To facilitate the execution of cyberspace operations, and to ensure proper command and control of the capabilities and organizations able to deliver effects in the conduct of these operations, the Department of Defense established the U.S. Cyber Command as a sub-unified command to U.S. Strategic Command in 2010. Commanded by General Keith Alexander, who is also the Director of the National Security Agency, U.S. Cyber Command is charged to not only defend Department of Defense information networks but also to conduct "full-spectrum military cyberspace operations (in accordance with all applicable laws and regulations) in order to ensure U.S. and allied freedom of action in cyberspace, while denying the same to our adversaries."[19] A year later, the Army stood up its service component headquarters, U.S. Army Cyber Command, and assigned responsibility for developing DOTMLPF requirements, capabilities, and solutions - as well as the mission of executing cyber operations – to the command.[20]

Both of these organizations, and the related organizations in the other military departments, were created to ensure the U.S. military retained freedom of maneuver in the cyberspace domain, and to ensure any potential adversaries did not have the same freedom. However, cyberspace operations are more than defending networks and attacking adversarial networks. Cyberspace operations are about the generation of effects: employing military capabilities both in and through the operational domain of cyberspace, and all its associated components, in order to create conditions favorable to the accomplishment of military objectives. For example, special operations forces use cyber capabilities to pinpoint the location of high value targets. Malicious code, such as the Stuxnet virus, can be inserted into adversary information systems to alter how machinery works. Viruses can be used to delete, change or manipulate the information needed to make decisions. These operations can consist of capabilities across the Army, but they are not the purview of one distinct branch or community. Additionally, they must be planned in support of an overarching operation – integration and synchronization are critical to the successful execution of cyberspace operations.

The Evolution of Information Operations

Following the experiences garnered during operations in the Persian Gulf War and the Balkans in the early 1990s, the U.S. military began exploring the need to develop a new strategy to combat an adversary's, and potential adversaries', use of the information environment. [21] In 1996, the Joint Staff published a new doctrine focused on the implementation of command and control warfare (C2W), "the integrated use of psychological operations (PSYOP), military deception, operations security (OPSEC), electronic warfare (EW), and physical destruction, mutually supported by intelligence, to deny information to, influence, degrade, or destroy adversary C2 capabilities while protecting friendly C2 capabilities against such actions."[22] Command and control warfare was further defined as a supporting tenet of Information Warfare – "actions taken to achieve information superiority by affecting adversary information, information-based processes, information systems, and computer-based networks while defending one's own information, information-based processes, information systems, and computer-based networks."[23] For the first time the U.S. military attempted to organize seemingly disparate functions and capabilities into a coordinating structure aimed at affecting the use of the information environment.

In August 1996, six months after the release of the joint doctrine on Command and Control Warfare, the Army released its own answer to the problem of how to create and manage effects in the information environment. Information Operations (FM 100-6) marked the first time the term was used in a doctrinal publication, and saw the association of Command and Control Warfare with Public Affairs and Civil Affairs as a means to affect the Global Information Environment.[24] However, the doctrine focused almost exclusively on attacking and exploiting adversarial information systems while protecting U.S. military information systems. This approach supported the efforts of the Land Information Warfare Activity, created by the United States Army Intelligence and Security Command (INSCOM) in 1994 as a new breed of intelligence organizations "designed to defend the Army's automated communications and data systems from outside intrusion and to give the Army full capabilities in both the defensive and offensive aspects of any future conflict in cyberspace."[25]

From 1996 until 2003, a debate raged inside the Army over the tenor of Information Operations (IO): was IO an intelligence function or an operational capability? Was it the execution of actions or the coordination of capabilities? What exactly were the core elements of IO? IO was viewed as the way of the future by many leaders, a means of insuring continued funding for Army capabilities. The resolution of this debate would give the "winner" a significant funding source for years to come. Although Army doctrinal publications are supposed to be reviewed and updated every two years, FM 100-6 did not receive a re-write during this period of discussion. When the revision appeared in 2003, it was as FM 3-13, Information Operations: Doctrine,

Tactics, Techniques and Procedures. As a result of the experiences derived from Operation Enduring Freedom and the fresh experiences of Operation Iraqi Freedom, the Army redefined IO:

> the employment of the core capabilities of electronic warfare, computer network operations, psychological operations, military deception, and operations security, in concert with specified supporting and related capabilities, to affect or defend information and information systems, and to influence decision making.[26]

In addition to recognizing the five capabilities that formed the core of Information Operations, the Army attempted to define the relationship of six supporting elements and two related activities to IO and how IO supported the operations process.[27] Most importantly, the Army formalized in doctrine, and later in organizational structure, the importance of IO by establishing a separate staff section – the G/S-7, Assistant Chief of Staff for Information Operations – responsible for planning, coordinating and synchronizing the capabilities incumbent to information operations into the operations process.[28]

Although the Army had made significant advances in codifying IO into its doctrine and formations, the effort failed to capture what IO meant to commanders. The doctrine continued to focus on IO as the evolution of command and control warfare focused on computer network operations, information systems (the protection of friendly systems, denying adversaries access to theirs), and network warfare. In the field, commanders began to view IO as the integration of all communication activities – activities and capabilities focused on informing, educating, inspiring, and influencing specific audiences. They recognized that, in order to succeed in their operations, denying their adversary freedom of movement in the information environment while simultaneously engaging key audiences in open, honest dialogue was critical.[29] Information Operations moved from a technical focus to focusing on behaviors, attitudes and perceptions. General Martin Dempsey, then the Commanding General of the U.S. Army Training and Doctrine Command, formally recognized this shift in focus in 2008 when, in his forward to the new Army Field Manual (FM) 3.0 Change 1, he announced that the Army would ""unburden the term information operations and regroup tasks under two headings: inform and influence activities (IIA) and cyber/electromagnetic activities."[30] The doctrine further recognized the critical importance of information to operations and the need to engage multiple audiences, not just adversaries:

> Information is a powerful tool in the operational environment. Information has become as important as lethal action in determining the outcome of operations. Every engagement, battle, and major operation requires complementary inform and influence activities to inform a global audience, to influence audiences, and to affect morale within the operational area.[31]

In 2009, General Stanley McChrystal, the new Commander of the International Security Assistance Forces (ISAF) in Afghanistan, charged his communication staff, led by Rear Admiral Greg Smith, to review the information environment in Afghanistan and develop recommendations for changes to communication structure, force allocation and programs. In their ISAF Communication Strategy, Admiral Smith's staff argued the strength of the coalition and the Government of Afghanistan lay in the perception of legitimacy. However, they did not stop with the Afghan population as the key audience.[32] They identified the U.S. and allied populations and governments as critical audiences that must be engaged in order to inform, educate and inspire so that the belief in legitimacy could be reinforced. This engagement became a continuous effort for General McChrystal and his staff. In a 2010 directive to all forces under his command, the ISAF Commander captured the critical importance of communicating with public audiences:

14

Public perception of ISAF and the Government of the Islamic Republic of Afghanistan (GIRoA) drives popular support, which is the most important element of reversing insurgent momentum in Afghanistan. Ultimately, we cannot secure the Afghan population or achieve GIRoA's governance and development goals without the population's active participation. Our ability to improve public perception (reinforced by the reality on the ground) and counter the enemy's harmful influence on public support is critical, particularly in the next 12 months. This makes communication a decisive effort.[33]

As in Iraq, the focus of Information Operations in Afghanistan moved from the medium – cyber, print, radio, etc. – to the audience and the message. The Army doctrinal development captured this shift in focus when, in September 2011, the Army unveiled FM 6-0, *Mission Command,* in which the commander was assigned the responsibility for conducting the two tasks that replaced Information Operations: Inform and Influence Activities and Cyber Electromagnetic Activities.[34]

Strategic Communication

Following the migration of Information Operations from a technically focused skill set to a capability focused on the application of soft power designed to generate effects in the information environment, several debates emerged among disparate interest groups. "Old school" IO professionals argued against the migration away from technical capabilities. Public Affairs officers argued that transforming into Inform and Influence Activities would undercut the trust and confidence in our public information necessary to ensure the American public and allied audiences supported our operations. Psychological Operations (now called Military Information Support Operations) professionals argued that IO was nothing more than Psychological Operations. Cyberspace operations practioneers argued that cyber capabilities must be developed separately from Inform and Influence Activities.

Out of this discourse grew a new debate over the concept of Strategic Communication. In October 2010, pursuant to Section 1055 of the Duncan Hunter National Defense Authorization Act for Fiscal Year 2009, President Barrack Obama defined Strategic Communication as "the synchronization of words and deeds and how they will be perceived by selected audiences, as well as programs and activities deliberately aimed at communicating and engaging with intended audiences, including those implemented by public affairs, public diplomacy, and information operations professionals." Strategic Communication is often thought of as something a government does – communicate to achieve a strategic outcome. However, President Obama was closer to reality when he emphasized "the synchronization of words and deeds," and "programs and activities deliberately aimed at communicating and engaging with intended audiences."[35] Strategic Communication is the synchronization of words and images with the actions and deeds of different capabilities to achieve a desired effect with an intended audience. That effect can be to inform, inspire, educate, or influence an individual's or a group's beliefs or actions. Strategic Communication is not a stand-alone capability that can exist outside an operational or decision making process; it must be fully integrated in order to ensure all actions are focused on the desired outcome.

In 2010, the President reported to Congress "Across all our efforts, effective strategic communications are essential to sustaining global legitimacy and supporting our policy aims."[36] Following the direction laid out in this report, and recognizing the need to better coordinate the actions of strategic communication (SC) capabilities, former Secretary of Defense Gates directed that Executive Agency for Information

Operations (IO) be moved from the Undersecretary of Defense for Intelligence to the Undersecretary of Defense for Policy (USD(P)), and he further directed that Executive Agency within the department for Strategic Communication be shared by USD(P) and the Assistant Secretary of Defense for Public Affairs.[37]

While these actions, along with the empowerment of the Global Engagement Strategy Coordination Committee (GESCC) to serve as the department's central coordinating body for SC, were a step in the right direction to better plan, coordinate, synchronize, execute, and assess the effects generated by not only the department's words but also its actions, they fell short in developing a communication capability that eliminates redundancy, increases efficiencies, consolidates responsibility under one chain of command, and produces integrated effects during a time period in which the department's budget will be under intense scrutiny. Even though both the President and former Secretary Gates espouse a cohesive, coordinated communication effort and community that synchronizes words with deeds across the government, the effort remains disjointed, primarily because of infighting among the three largest members of the communication community: Public Affairs (PA), IO and Psychological Operations (PSYOP).

The confusion over the roles, responsibilities, and authorities of the communication community is rooted in the passage of the Smith-Mundt Act of 1948. Usually misquoted for the purpose of establishing a barrier between PSYOP and PA capabilities, the Smith-Mundt Act simply granted the State Department the authorities necessary to disseminate information abroad, and it banned the State Department from disseminating information inside America or to American citizens.[38] Each year, the

Defense Authorization Act includes a stipulation against the department conducting propaganda activities within the United States. There is no legislation preventing the integration of communication capabilities to achieve desired effects with specific audiences. In fact, one could argue that these capabilities are already integrated under one office – either the Secretary of Defense or a designated Commander already has the authority and responsibility to integrate these capabilities. However, the stigma of the short-lived Office of Strategic Influence from the early days of 2002 has served to limit the integration and joining of capabilities to achieve effects in the communication world.[39] To this day, despite presidential emphasis and congressional requirements, the department is unable to synchronize from top to bottom ongoing actions of communication capabilities in support of national security objectives nor is it able to adequately account for spending, often duplicative, among competing communication communities.

Current Trends in the Application of Information

IN 2009, when he assumed command of the International Security Assistance Forces – Afghanistan (ISAF) and U.S. Forces Afghanistan (USFOR-A), General Stanley McChrystal inherited a communication apparatus that was so disparate that it was dysfunctional. ISAF capabilities and authorities were planned, coordinated and executed in a vacuum, completely separate from USFOR-A capabilities and authorities. Direct engagements were planned in isolation by a team reporting to the ISAF Chief of Staff or to the USFOR-A Deputy Commander – by a completely separate team –for congressional delegation and other U.S.-only VIP visits. Public Affairs activities were conducted in a reactive-centric media operations center reporting to the Director of Public Affairs, and tactical PSYOP activities were coordinated under the auspices of the

Information Operations Director, who reported to the CJ-3. No coordination mechanism existed to ensure synchronization of messages and actions.

General McChrystal established a unified command structure in which all communication capabilities – Direct Engagement (similar to Public Support to Public Diplomacy), IO, PSYOP, and PA (both Command Information and Media Operations activities) – were under the direction of a Deputy Chief of Staff for Communication (DCOS COMM). The Communication Directorate included a planning element that was embedded with the U.S. Embassy, General McChrystal's Strategic Advisory Group (SAG), the CJ-5 planning group, and across the other functional areas of ISAF. It even included an assessment and media monitoring capability. Although this construct was a severe deviation from established NATO doctrine, and U.S. Joint Doctrine, NATO – from Secretary General Anders Fogh Rasmussen down – quickly endorsed this construct because for the first time all communication capabilities were working together, side-by-side, coordinating and synchronizing messaging actions with deeds on the ground. This organizational structure was so successful that in 2010 The RAND Corporation - in a report commissioned by the French Joint Forces Centre for Concept Development, Doctrine, and Experimentation – recommended that France adopt this model to develop its national strategic communication structure and capability.[40]

The Way Ahead

In announcing the new National Defense Strategy, President Obama identified a strong U.S. economy as the foundation of our strength around the globe. In this era of budget constraints, the Department of Defense must eliminate duplication of efforts and increase efficiencies. The Army can accomplish this by accepting the importance of information as an element of power and by accepting the relationship of the cyber domain to both the other operational domains and to the information environment. In this and future eras of fiscal constraints, the Army cannot afford to approach the problem of how to conduct operations in the information environment in the same archaic manner in which it has up to this point.

Following the War of 1812, the U.S. Army opened the first branch schools to better serve the educational needs of a professional force.[41] Ever since that point in history Army branches have worked to protect their niche, ensure their viability, protect their capabilities, and find new means to grow for the future force. The Army cannot afford to continue this business practice, and the debate that surrounds Information and Cyberspace is the ideal situation for the Army to break the barriers set by the branch and functional area structure.

The branches of the Army are organized to deliver effects, or enable the delivery of effects, in the physical domains only. It is because of this that the current branch structure is ill-suited to meet the needs of commanders in the complex operating environment. Cyberspace, as previously discussed, is the medium through which, and in which, a commander can create effects that ensure the ability to use data and affect an adversary's ability to use his data. However, the cyberspace domain is not a stand-alone entity – it exists within the information environment. Just as with the debate in the IO community over who "owned" IO, the debate among the disparate communities has focused on lead, or primacy, for capabilities. What has been absent is a discussion on how these capabilities fit together in order to meet the effects-delivery needs of the commander.

Globalization, as previously noted, has led to the rise in importance of information as an element of national power. As a result, strategic leader across the government have identified the imperative to communicate with specific audiences – for the purposes of informing, educating, persuading, inspiring, and influence.[42] As the Army weighs where to make cuts in order to meet the fiscal constraints demanded by Congress and the guidance provided by the Secretary of Defense, it is critical to examine how we deliver communication capabilities and capacity for commanders.

There are only so many means of communicating with specific audiences. You can communicate face-to-face through leader and soldier engagements. You can broadcast radio, television, and internet content. You can distribute written material, either directly to the audience or through a secondary source. Or you can provide access to information so a trusted agent, such as the media or intermediary, can make an informed decision and relay your information. However, the Army is bifurcating its communication effort through the branch process. The Army continues to promulgate the belief that Public Affairs, Information Operations, and Military Information Support Operations (formerly Psychological Operations) deliver unique capabilities. In reality, they perform the same function: they communicate with intended audiences. What differentiates them is the audience with whom they communicate (U.S. vs. adversary, allied vs. host nation, etc.) and the effect they strive to achieve (Inform, Educate, Inspire, Persuade, or Influence). Contrary to popular belief, the media is not an intended audience; it is a medium through which a commander can reach a specific audience based on detailed target audience analysis – determining who you need to affect and how they best receive and process information. The Army can no longer afford to maintain the DOTMLPF ramifications for these three distinct career fields, all performing the same function.

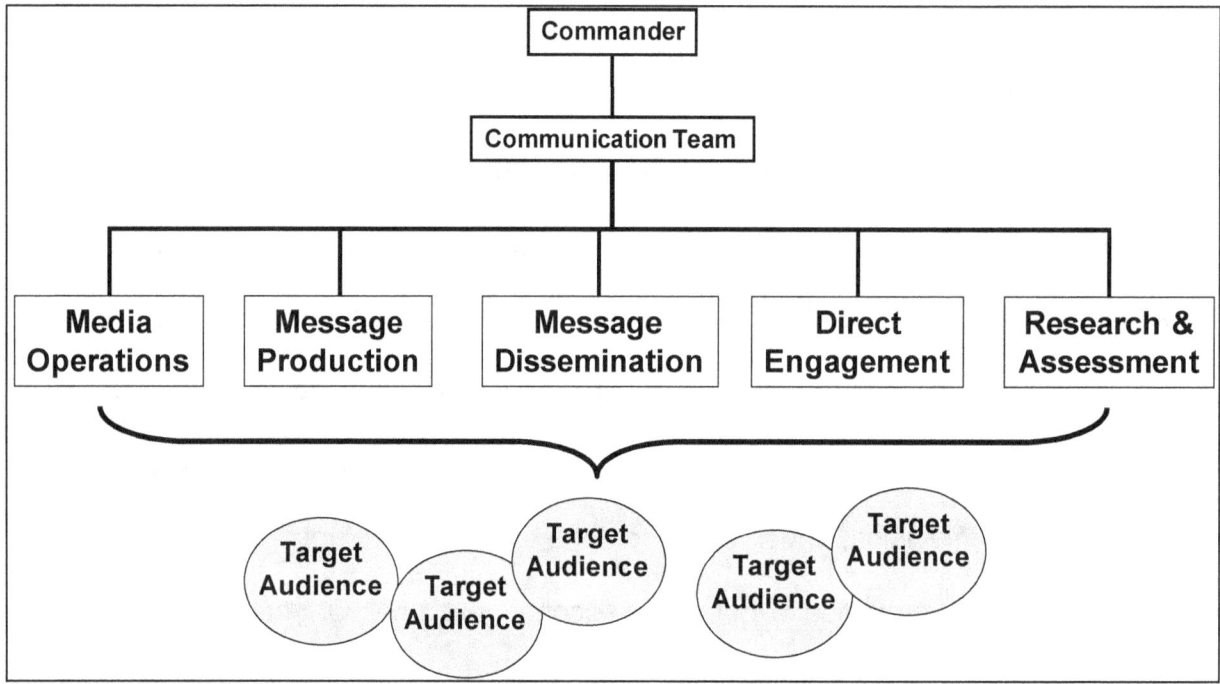

Figure 2. Communication Effects Organized by Function, not Target Audience or Career Field bias

Figure two is an elementary illustration of how the Army can gain efficiencies and improve coordination and synchronization by combining communication capabilities, similar to the ISAF model outlined above, to focus on functional roles as opposed to audiences. It is essential to maintain a separate media operations function to ensure the Army does not violate any applicable laws or regulations.

The emergence of cyberspace as an operational domain, coupled with the effect globalization has had on the increased importance of information as an element of national power places the Army at a unique juncture in time. It can continue to allow a capabilities development process founded on history to attempt to meet the needs of commanders, often coming short of the need and causing commander's to adapt as they best see fit. Or the Army can seize this opportunity to re-energize its ability to provide commander's the tools essential to deliver effects in increasingly complex and ambiguous operational environments. Just as it is time to combine capabilities that perform the same functions in the communication realm, it is time to combine capabilities in the cyber-electromagnetic community. Figure three portrays one method for combining functions in a new cyber-electromagnetic career field to better serve the needs of commanders.

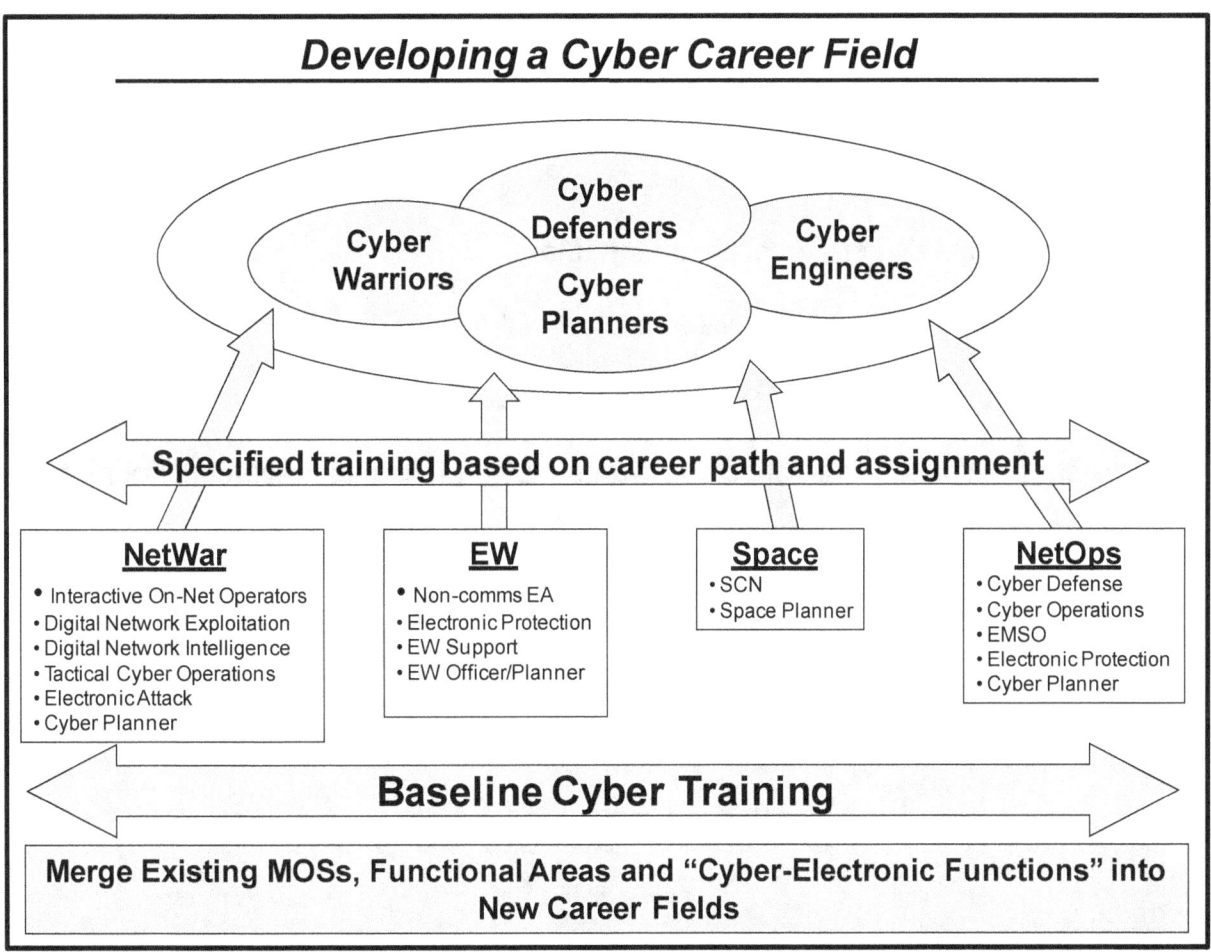

Figure 3. Proposed realignment for Cyber-Electromagnetic Career Field

As the Army determines how best to develop, and retain, the capabilities essential to providing for the defense of the nation, the Army must be willing to do so in an intellectual environment unencumbered by traditional branch biases. Neither communication effects nor cyberspace effects are a subset of Information Operations. Communicators can create effects in the cyberspace domain just as they can in the physical domains, and commanders can create communication effects with maneuver forces in the information environment and cyberspace just as they do in the physical domains. By combining capabilities that perform similar functions into two capability development fields, Cyberspace and Communication, the Army will be better postured to deliver the effects necessary to conduct successful operations in all domains. While the Army grows the force necessary to fill these two capability fields, professionals currently serving in the feeder career fields can be aligned with the area with which they have the most expertise or are most comfortable.

If the military is to remain a viable element of national power, it is imperative that it changes the manner in which it develops, manages, coordinates, synchronizes, and employs capabilities to create effects in cyberspace and the information environment. The changes in the global environment and the manner in which we as a nation employ national power necessitate that we re-examine our approach to communication. Failure to do so may leave the Army in a position where it is unable to meet the needs of the nation.

Endnotes

[1] Ronald Reagan, quoted in *The Guardian (London)*, June 14, 1989, http://en.wikiquote.org/wiki/Liberty (accessed on February 26, 2012).

[2] Carl von Clausewitz, *On War*, 1St Edition ed. (Minneapolis, MN: Princeton University Press, 1989), 77.

[3] Ibid, 75.

[4] Ibid, 607

[5] Alvin Toeffler, *The Third Wave,* (New York, NY: Morrow, 1980), 38.

[6] Kenneth Osgood, *Total Cold War: Eisenhower's Secret Propaganda Battle at Home and Abroad* (Lawrence, KS: University Press of Kansas, 2006), 47.

[7] Dwight Eisenhower, "Farewell Address," January 17, 1961, http://www.ourdocuments.gov/doc.php?doc=90&page=transcript (accessed February 11, 2012).

[8] Barrack Obama, "Defense Strategic Guidance Briefing from the Pentagon," *U.S. Department of Defense News Transcript* (January 5, 2012).

[9] Toeffler, 27.

[10] Leon Panetta, *Sustaining U.S. Global Leadership: Priorities for 21st Century Defense* (Washington, DC: U.S. Department of Defense, January 2012), 2.

[11] Barack Obama, *National Security Strategy* (Washington, DC: The White House, May 2010), 1.

[12] Leon Panetta, 3.

[13] Uzi Mahnaimi and Sarah Baxter, "Revealed: Israel plans nuclear strike on Iran." The London Times, Jan 07, 2007, The Sunday Times section, http://www.commondreams.org/headlines07/0107-04.htm (accessed February 25, 2012).

[14] Robert McMillan, "Was Stuxnet Built to Attack Iran's Nuclear Program?." PC World, Sept 21, 2010, http://www.pcworld.com/businesscenter/article/205827/was_stuxnet_built_to_attack_irans_nuclear_program.html (accessed September 20, 2011).

[15] Deputy Secretary of Defense Gordon England, "The Definition of 'Cyberspace'," memorandum for Secretaries of the Military Departments, Washington, DC, May 12, 2008.

[16] Vice Chairman of the Joint Chiefs of Staff James Cartwright, "Definition of Cyberspace Operations," memorandum for Deputy Secretary of Defense, Washington, DC, September 29, 2008.

[17] George W. Bush, *The National Strategy to Secure Cyberspace* (Washington, DC: The White House, February 2003), 1.

[18] Robert M. Gates, *National Military Strategy for Cyberspace Operations,* (Washington, DC: U.S. Department of Defense, 2006), 2.

[19] U.S. Strategic Command, "U.S. Cyberspace Command Fact Sheet," http://www.stratcom.mil/factsheets/cyber_command/ (accessed January 21, 2012).

[20] U.S. Army Cyber Command, "Army Cyber Command History," http://www.arcyber.army.mil/org-arcyber.html (accessed January 21, 2012).

[21] Christopher Paul *Information Operations Doctrine and Practice* (Westport, CT: Praeger Security International, 2008), 2.

[22] U.S. Joint Chiefs of Staff, *Joint Doctrine for Command and Control Warfare (C2W),* Joint Publication 3-13.1 (Washington, DC: U.S. Joint Chiefs of Staff, 1996), I-4.

[23] JP 3-13.1, 1996, I-3.

[24] U.S. Department of the Army, *Information Operations,* Field Manual 100-6 (Washington, DC: U.S. Department of the Army, 1996), 2-3

[25] U.S. Army Intelligence and Security Command, "The INSCOM Story Continued …," January 11, 2012, http://www.inscom.army.mil/Organization/History_supp.aspx?text=off&size=12pt, accessed January 21, 2012.

[26] U.S. Department of the Army, *Information Operations: Doctrine, Tactics, Techniques, and Procedures,* Field Manual 3-13 (Washington, DC: U.S. Department of the Army, 2003), 1-13.

[27] FM 3-13 defined the core elements of IO as Computer Network Operations (CNO), Electronic Warfare (EW), Military Deception, Psychological Operations (PSYOP), and Operational Security (OPSEC). The supporting elements were Physical Destruction, Information Assurance (IA), Physical Security, Counterintelligence, Counterdeception, and Counterpropaganda. The capabilities of Public Affairs (PA) and Civil Affairs (CA), included in the 1996 doctrine, were moved from supporting elements to related activities in the new publication as a result of protests from the PA and CA communities.

[28] FM 3-13, 1-21.

[29] LTG Thomas Metz et al, "Massing Effects in the Information Domain: A Case Study in Aggressive Information Operations," in *Ideas as Weapons,* ed. G.J. David Jr. and T.R. McKeldin III (Washington, DC: Potomac Books, 2009), 267.

[30] U.S. Department of the Army, *Operations,* Field Manual 3.0 Change 1 (Washington, DC: U.S. Department of the Army, February 2008), forward.

[31] FM 3.0, Change 1, 4-3.

[32] From 2009-2010, the author was the Deputy Director for Communication on the ISAF staff, responsible for developing the communication strategy, structure, and capability required to support the ISAF mission. LTC John Gallagher and he were the principle authors of the communication strategy for RADM Smith and GEN McChrystal.

[33] ISAF Commander General Stanley McChrystal, "COMISAF Communication Directive," Commander's Directive for all subordinate forces, Kabul, Afghanistan, March 1, 2010

[34] U.S. Department of the Army, *Mission Command*, Field Manual 6-0 (Washington, DC: U.S. Department of the Army, September 2011), 2-7.

[35] Barack H. Obama, *National Framework for Strategic Communication* (Washington, DC: The White House, 2010), 1.

[36] Ibid, 1.

[37] U.S. Secretary of Defense Robert M. Gates, "Strategic Communication and Information Operations in the DoD," Memorandum for Secretaries of the Military Departments et al, Washington, DC, January 25, 2011.

[38] Matt Armstrong, "Smith-Mundt Act: Facts, Myths, and Recommendations," nd, http://mountainrunner.us/smith-mundt.html#factmyths (accessed November 12, 2011).

[39] Secretary of Defense Donald Rumsfeld established the Office of Strategic Defense immediately following the attacks on 9/11. The office's stated purpose was to synchronize departmental efforts to mislead adversaries and foreign audiences about U.S. intentions and capabilities. An intense debate in the U.S. media over the morality of using the U.S. media as a tool for deception, and Secretary Rumsfeld was forced to close the office in 2002.

[40] Anaïs Reding, Kristin Weed, and Jeremy J. Ghez, *NATO's Strategic Communications concept and its relevance for France* (Santa Monica, CA: The RAND Corporation, 2010), 35-36.

[41] The Center of Military History, *American Military History, Volume I: The United States Army and the Forging of a Nation, 1775-1917,* ed. Richard W. Stewart (Washington, DC: U.S. Army Center of Military History, 2005), 174.

[42] Obama, *National Framework for Strategic Communication,* 1.